KEEPING YOUR TEETH CLEAN

by Nicole A. Mansfield

PEBBLE
a capstone imprint

Published by Pebble, an imprint of Capstone
1710 Roe Crest Drive, North Mankato, Minnesota 56003
capstonepub.com

Library of Congress Cataloging-in-Publication Data is available on the Library of Congress website.

ISBN: 9780756571160 (hardcover)
ISBN: 9780756571122 (paperback)
ISBN: 9780756570927 (ebook PDF)

Summary: We have all kinds of bacteria in our mouths. Some are good for us. Others are not. What can you do to help keep the bad bacteria off your teeth? Find out in this book.

Editorial Credits
Editor: Ericka Smith; Designer: Sarah Bennett; Media Researcher: Svetlana Zhurkin; Production Specialist: Katy LaVigne

Consultant Credits
Patricia V. Hermanson, DMD, MS

Image Credits
Getty Images: Artfoliophoto, 15, Daniel Pangbourne, 19, Jose Luis Pelaez Inc, 9, PeopleImages, 12, PhotoAlto/James Hardy, 7, Science Photo Library, 6 (inset); Shutterstock: AAraujo, 14, Africa Studio, 20, Brian A Smith, 17, CGN089, 16, DC Studio, 6, Designifty, 1 (smiling tooth), ilusmedical, 10 (inset), jpreat, 8, Mark Janus, cover, Maxx-Studio, 4, Monkey Business Images, 18, nalinda117, 11, Nina Buday, 5, Perfectorius, cover (design elements), poonsap, 19, Rvector (background), 3, 22–23, 24, Vanatchanan, 10, wavebreakmedia, 13, Zhanna Markina (background), cover, back cover, and throughout

All internet sites appearing in back matter were available and accurate when this book was sent to press.

Printed and bound in China. 5130

Table of Contents

Words in **bold** are in the glossary.

Clean Is Cool

You have more than 300 kinds of **bacteria** in your mouth. That's a lot! Some are good. And some are bad.

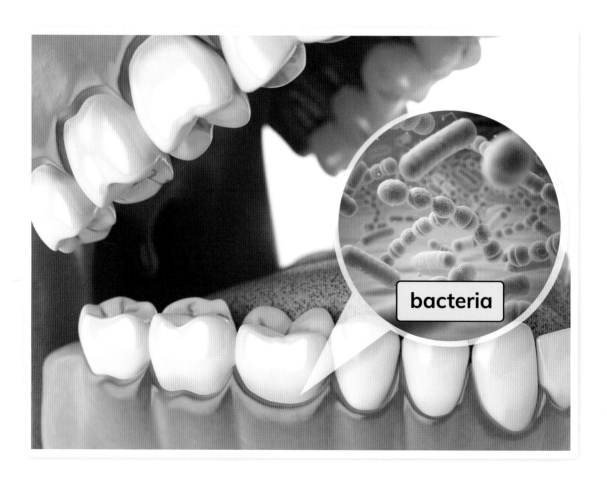

bacteria

You can beat the bad bacteria. You just have to keep your teeth clean!

What Is Bacteria?

Everyone has bacteria in their mouth. Bacteria are tiny living things. You need a **microscope** to see them!

Good bacteria help break down food. They help keep your mouth clean. And they help fight bad bacteria. Bad bacteria can cause problems when you eat sugary foods.

What Is Plaque?

Have you ever felt something sticky on your teeth? That's **plaque**. Everyone has it.

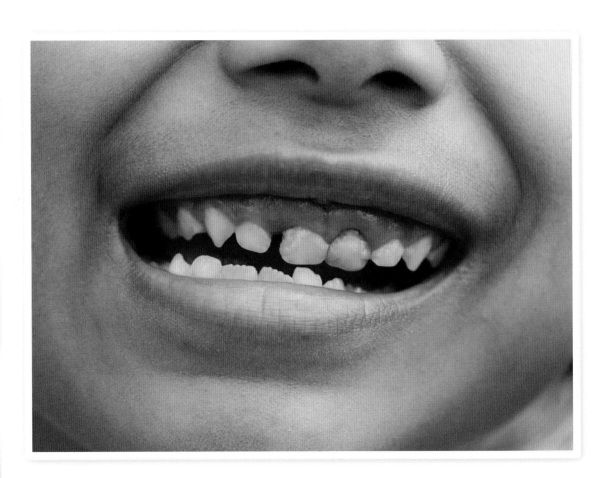

When you eat, bits of food stick to your teeth. Bacteria, **saliva**, and food mix to make plaque. The bacteria in plaque can create **acid** too.

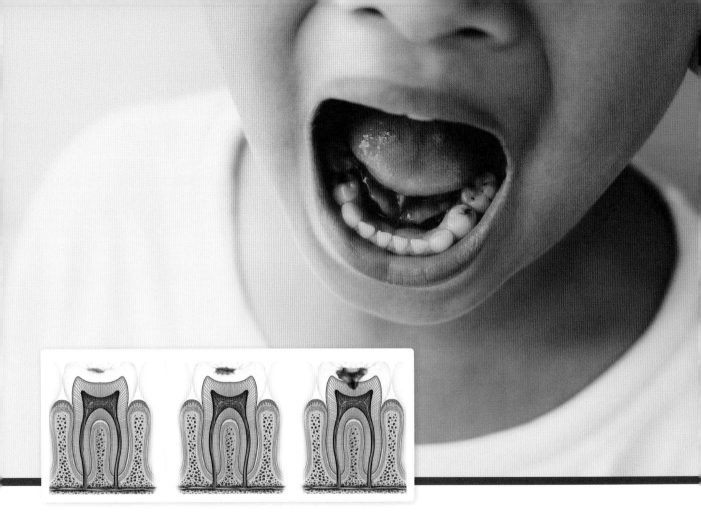

Your teeth are coated in **enamel**. Enamel
helps protect the soft parts inside your teeth.
Acid can harm your enamel. It can make holes
in your teeth. Those holes are called **cavities**.

Plaque can also cause bad breath.
It can lead to **gum** disease. Gum disease
is damage to the parts around your teeth.
Plaque makes your teeth look yellow too.

Brush Away the Bad Guys!

You can say goodbye to these bad bacteria! You do that by brushing your teeth every morning and every night.

First, rinse your mouth with water. Next, put a pea-sized amount of toothpaste on a toothbrush. Brush with short **strokes**. But don't brush too hard!

Bacteria live on your tongue too. They can cause bad breath. Gently brush your tongue to get rid of them.

Set a timer for two minutes. That's how long you need to brush your teeth and tongue. Then, spit out the toothpaste. Rinse your mouth and your toothbrush.

Don't Forget to Floss

Floss once a day. It helps remove plaque. Get a piece of floss about as long as your arm. Wind it around your middle fingers. Leave an inch of floss between them.

Slide the floss between two teeth. Make a C shape around one tooth. Move the floss up and down. Repeat for the other tooth. Pull the floss out. Move to the next two teeth!

Keep Your Teeth Clean

Keeping your teeth clean is a big job. First, be careful about what you eat. Don't eat too many sweets or drink too much soda and juice. And eat lots of vegetables.

Then, remember to brush twice a day. And floss once a day. With practice, you'll be a pro at it!

Healthy Teeth Collage

A collage is a group of pictures and words that shows an idea. You know a lot about how to keep your teeth healthy, so let's make a healthy teeth collage. Ask an adult to help you.

What You Need

- health magazines, weekly store ads, and coupon books

- scissors

- glue

- 1 large poster board

- markers

What You Do

1. Look through the magazines, ads, and coupons. Cut out pictures of foods that are good for your teeth. Fruits and vegetables are good examples. Then, cut out pictures of toothbrushes, toothpaste, floss, people brushing their teeth, and people smiling!

2. Glue the pictures onto the poster board.

3. Use markers to add words and phrases about keeping your teeth clean to your collage.

Show your collage to your family and friends! Tell them what you've learned about keeping your teeth clean.

Glossary

acid (A-suhd)—a strong liquid

bacteria (bak-TEER-ee-uh)—very small living things that exist everywhere in nature

cavity (KAV-uh-tee)—a hole in a tooth, caused by the acid bateria produce

enamel (ih-NAM-uhl)—the hard outer surface of a tooth

gum (GUHM)—the firm flesh around the base of a person's tooth

microscope (MYE-kruh-skope)—a tool that makes very small things look large enough to be seen

plaque (PLAK)—the coating of food, saliva, and bacteria that forms on teeth and can cause tooth decay

saliva (suh-LYE-vuh)—the clear liquid in the mouth

stroke (STROHK)—a complete movement

Read More

Clark, Rosalyn. *Why We Go to the Dentist.* Minneapolis: Lerner Publications, 2018.

Rustad, E. H. *Care for Your Teeth.* North Mankato, MN: Capstone, 2021.

Simmons, Caressa. *Why Do I Need to Brush My Teeth?* Edison, GA: Jubilant World Books, 2021.

Internet Sites

KidsHealth: Taking Care of Your Teeth
kidshealth.org/en/kids/teeth-care.html

Mouth Healthy: 5 Reasons Your Smile Is Stronger Than You Think
mouthhealthy.org/en/fun-teeth-facts-part-2

YouTube: How to Brush Teeth Correctly (Colgate)
youtube.com/watch?v=1q10LWifXkw

Index

About the Author

Nicole A. Mansfield dedicates all of her children's books to her own three children—Victorious, Justine, and Zion. She lives in Georgia and is passionate about singing at her church. Nicole loves to take long walks with her kids and her active-duty military husband of 19 years.